Aug. '96

To   Anne Wilso

D1396543

Enjoy the "Newfie"
Cuisine & pictorial beauty.
of our most Eastern
Province.

Your friend
Bev ☺

NEWFOUNDLAND Pictorial Cookbook

Photographs by Sherman Hines

Introduction and Recipes
by Al Clouston

NIMBUS PUBLISHING LIMITED

Nimbus Publishing Limited
P.O. Box 9301, Station A
Halifax, Nova Scotia
B3K 5N5

Design: Arthur Carter, Halifax

Cameras: Pentax 6x7 and Contax with Carl Zeiss T lens
Film: Fujichrome

All photographs available from:
Master File
Stock Photo Library
415 Yonge Street, Suite 200
Toronto, Ontario
M5B 2E7

Canadian Cataloguing in Publication Data

Hines, Sherman, 1941-

Newfoundland pictorial cookbook

ISBN 0-921054-43-2

1. Cookery, Canadian— Newfoundland style.
2. Newfoundland— Description and travel— Views
I. Title.

TX715.6.H56 1990 641.59718 c90-097540-7

Printed and bound in Hong Kong

Cover: A good day for fishing
Back cover: Puffin
Title page: St. John's
Table of Contents: Typical foggy day
Introduction: Docked in the harbour

Table of Contents

Introduction

By Al Clouston

Newfoundland was settled centuries ago by immigrants from England, Ireland, Scotland and, later, mainland Canada. Because the island was so isolated and the communities spread so far apart, people had to become self-sufficient, doing their own fishing, farming, hunting, and berry picking.

Until World War II, fridges, electric stoves, and deep-freezers were almost unheard of; wood-stoves were the norm for most people. Codfish, herring, mackerel, and caplin were salted and sun dried or stored in barrels. Even turrs were preserved by salting. Vegetables from gardens were kept in root cellars dug in the ground or under houses. Given the rocky soil and the short growing season, potatoes, carrots, turnips, cabbages, and beets were typical crops. Wild berries such as partridgeberries were stored in barrels of water so that they lasted over the winter. Blueberries and bake-apples— called "cloudberries" in Scandinavia— were bottled for later use.

In fact, people had to stock up for the winter. They bought flour and apples and salt beef by the barrel, butter in wooden tubs, sugar in bales, molasses in puncheons, and cheese in wooden boxes. They also bought baking goods and dried fruit for Christmas and Easter.

Many products were scarce— milk, for example. Canned milk was used in tea, coffee, cooking, and for feeding babies. Some people did have cows, and most had a few chickens for eggs. Pigs were raised and then killed in the fall, when the weather turned cold. Sheep were another source of fresh meat.

Obviously, life was not easy. Women stayed in the home while men went out fishing or logging. Water had to be carried from the well, and wood had to be brought in for the fire; clothes were washed by hand or boiled on the wood-stove. As well, kerosene lamps had to be cleaned and lit, stoves had to be stoked, and fish had to be put out on flakes and brought in in the evening.

The shortage of certain kinds of foods and the lifestyle led to the development of unique Newfoundland dishes and culinary traditions. Many Newfoundlanders had special days for specific meals. Monday was "leftover day," Wednesday and Friday were "fish" days, Saturday was "pea-soup and baked-beans day," and Sunday was "fresh-meat day."

One favourite "scoff" was Jiggs dinner. Salt beef was cut up and soaked in cold water overnight. Then it was cooked for several hours, and potatoes, carrots, turnips, parsnips, and cabbage were added. The finishing touch was

peas pudding, split peas tied in a muslin bag and cooked with the meat.

There was nothing more Newfoundland than fisherman's brewis. "Brewis," hard bread or oval-shaped biscuits, was soaked overnight and then brought to a boil. Then it was chopped and served with fresh or salted cod and "scruncheons," small chunks of fried-out fat-back pork. Brewis was not always served with fish. Topped with sugar and butter, it was relished as an accompaniment to Sunday breakfast.

Many other traditional recipes, such as steamed puddings or steamed duffs (served with vegetables), called for fat-back pork, as well as molasses. Molasses also made candies called "bull's eyes," which were a treat for children. Molasses was boiled to the hard-ball stage and cooled. Then children greased their hands and pulled the taffy until it became creamy in colour.

In addition to Jiggs dinner, steamed duffs, and fisherman's brewis, many traditional dishes are still enjoyed as much as ever. Rabbit stew or cooked rabbit served with gravy and vegetables is popular. Rabbits have always been plentiful in Newfoundland. One year, however, they were scarce, and there was a ban on selling them. The Newfoundland Rangers were the law keepers at that time, and one ranger went to investigate a rumour that a fellow was selling rabbits. When he arrived on the scene, he discovered that the rabbit catcher had quite a supply on hand. After a short conversation, the ranger asked the man to sell him a brace. "No, zir," the man said, "'tis agin' the law, but I'll give eh a pair." The man disappeared and in short order returned with the rabbits, all skinned and cleaned. "Dere you are, zir. All I wants is 50 cents apiece for cleanin' 'em."

No true Newfoundlander ever turns down a plate of cod tongues, one of the "national" dishes. Cod tongues should always be fried and well browned in rendered-out fat-back pork.

People still rely partly on wild berries for fruit. Blueberries and partridgeberries are the most prolific, and pies filled with either can't be equalled. When people are "making over" the hills with a basket or a bucket in their hands, they are going "burry pickin'." Once, a post-office clerk was addressing a parcel for a fellow:

Clerk: To whom is this parcel going?
Customer: John Burry
Clerk: Who is the sender?
Customer: Bill Burry
Clerk: What is in the parcel?
Customer: Burries.

Al Clouston has published several books of Newfoundland humour, as well as a collection of Newfoundland recipes. He lives in St. John's.

Herring is caught off the Gulf and south shores of Newfoundland. Pickled herring makes a terrific snack or appetizer.

Pickled Herring

Salt herring
Cold water
Several onions
1 qt (1 L) malt vinegar
2 tbsp (25 mL) pickling spices
3/4 cup (175 mL) water
1/3 to 1/2 cup (75 mL to 125 mL)
   sugar

Clean and fillet salt herring. Soak in cold water. Drain, skin, and cut into bite-size pieces. Slice onions medium thin. Loosely layer herring and onions in sterilized wide-neck jars. Combine malt vinegar, pickling spices, 3/4 cup (175 mL) water, and sugar. Stir well and simmer for 10 minutes. Cool mixture and pour over herring, covering well. Seal and store in a cool place.

Note: Cool pickling sauce. If hot, it will soften herring.

Photo: Ramea, south coast
Overleaf: St. Anthony's, Great Northern Peninsula

7

This is one of the great Newfoundland recipes. Use small cod tongues because larger ones have more fat.

Fried Cod Tongues

5 lb (2.5 kg) fresh cod tongues
1 lb (500 g) fat-back pork, cut into
   scruncheons (small cubes)
1 lb (500 g) flour
Salt to taste
White pepper to taste

Wash cod tongues. Drain but do not dry. Fry out scruncheons and remove from skillet when crispy. Combine flour, salt, and pepper. Drop in cod tongues and toss lightly. Fry tongues lightly in same skillet as fat-back pork. Turn over tongues and add fried scruncheons while tongues finish cooking.

Photo: Brigus, Conception Bay

11

Fisherman's brewis is common all over Newfoundland.

Fisherman's Brewis

4 cakes hard bread
Cold water
1 tsp (5 mL) salt
Saltfish
Fat-back pork, chopped

Soak hard bread overnight in plenty of cold water. Drain next morning and add more water. Add salt and bring to a boil. Boil for 5 minutes. Drain bread until very dry. Boil saltfish, which has been soaking for several hours. Drain fish and add to bread; chop together well. Fry out fat-back pork and serve over brewis.
Photo: A happy fisherman

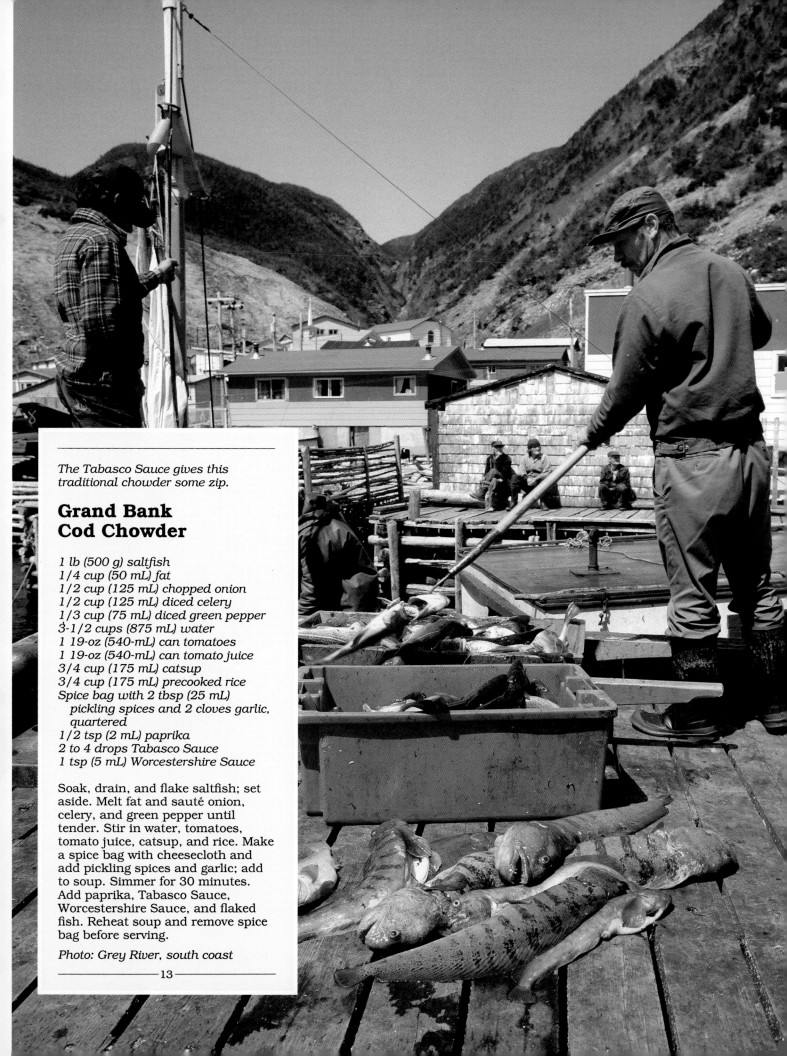

The Tabasco Sauce gives this traditional chowder some zip.

Grand Bank Cod Chowder

1 lb (500 g) saltfish
1/4 cup (50 mL) fat
1/2 cup (125 mL) chopped onion
1/2 cup (125 mL) diced celery
1/3 cup (75 mL) diced green pepper
3-1/2 cups (875 mL) water
1 19-oz (540-mL) can tomatoes
1 19-oz (540-mL) can tomato juice
3/4 cup (175 mL) catsup
3/4 cup (175 mL) precooked rice
Spice bag with 2 tbsp (25 mL)
    pickling spices and 2 cloves garlic,
    quartered
1/2 tsp (2 mL) paprika
2 to 4 drops Tabasco Sauce
1 tsp (5 mL) Worcestershire Sauce

Soak, drain, and flake saltfish; set aside. Melt fat and sauté onion, celery, and green pepper until tender. Stir in water, tomatoes, tomato juice, catsup, and rice. Make a spice bag with cheesecloth and add pickling spices and garlic; add to soup. Simmer for 30 minutes. Add paprika, Tabasco Sauce, Worcestershire Sauce, and flaked fish. Reheat soup and remove spice bag before serving.

Photo: Grey River, south coast

13

These are suitable for breakfast or lunch, using up leftover fish and potatoes.

Bonavista Fish Cakes

1 cup (250 mL) cod, cooked and flaked
1-1/2 cups (375 mL) mashed potatoes
1 tsp (5 mL) finely chopped onion
Salt to taste
Oil for frying

Blend together fish, mashed potatoes, and onion. Add salt. Divide into 6 equal portions, form balls, and pat into cakes. Fry cakes in a hot greased skillet until golden brown on both sides.

Note: If desired, substitute saltfish. First, soak overnight and cover with fresh cold water and boil for 20 minutes. Omit salt from recipe.

Photo: Filleting cod, St. John's

Partridge *is a rough term that refers to different kinds of grouse. In Newfoundland it is usually ptarmigan.*

Roast Partridge

Brace partridge
1-1/2 cups (375 mL) bread crumbs
1-1/2 tsp (7 mL) dried savory
1-1/2 tbsp (20 mL) butter
1 tsp (5 mL) chopped onion
Salt
Pepper
Bacon

Clean partridge. Combine bread crumbs, savory, butter, and onion; stuff partridge. Arrange stuffed partridge on a baking pan and season with salt and pepper. Lay 3 strips bacon over each partridge and bake at 350°F (180°C) until tender.

Photo: Partridge

Moose are not indigenous to the province: they were imported early in this century. Nonetheless, moose dishes have become favourite fare. Let the meat age for 7 to 10 days and remove the membrane before cooking.

Moose Stew

1/4 lb (125 g) butter
3 lb (1.5 kg) moose, cut into chunks
6 cups (1.5 L) water
Salt to taste
Pepper to taste
1 onion, chopped

2 carrots
2 parsnips
1 small turnip
6 potatoes

Melt butter and fry moose meat until browned. Add water, salt, and pepper. Simmer for 30 minutes and add onion. Simmer for another hour. Peel and cut up carrots, parsnips, turnip, and potatoes; add to stew. Simmer stew for 30 minutes or until vegetables are tender. If desired, make favourite dumplings.

Photo: Moose

By and large, rabbits are snared, not shot. In fall and winter, traps can be found along the edges of forests. Serve rabbit pie with potatoes, green peas, or other vegetables.

Broadcove Rabbit Pie

Brace fresh rabbits
Fat-back pork
1 large onion, chopped
1 medium carrot, chopped
1 small parsnip, sliced
1 medium-size turnip, diced
Water
Pastry

Skin and dress rabbits and cut into sections. Fry out several rashers of fat-back pork. Fry legs and thick back sections of rabbits until nicely browned. Remove from heat and add onion, carrot, parsnip, and turnip. Add water until covered and bake at 350°F (180°C) until meat comes away readily from bone. Add water if necessary. Cover with a not-too-rich pastry and bake until lightly browned.

Photo: Houses on rocky hills

The best word to describe flipper dinner is rich. The key to making this dish is to clean all the fat off the seal meat before cooking.

Labrador Flipper Dinner

2 lb (1 kg) seal meat
Water
2 tbsp (25 mL) vinegar
3 slices fat-back pork
Salt to taste
Pepper to taste
1 onion, sliced
1 large carrot, sliced
1 turnip, cubed
2 tbsp (25 mL) screech
3 cups (750 mL) water
Flour
Pastry:
1 cup (250 mL) flour
1-1/2 tsp (7 mL) baking powder
1 tbsp (15 mL) margarine or butter
1 egg, beaten
1/2 cup (125 mL) water

Place meat in a bowl and add water and vinegar to cover. Let sit for 1 hour; remove meat and dry well. Fry meat in fat-back pork, turning until browned on both sides. Add salt, pepper, and onion. Cover and simmer for 1 hour. Place carrot and turnip around meat. Add screech and 3 cups (750 mL) water. Cover and bake at 300°F (150°C) for 1 hour, adding mixture of flour and water to thicken if desired. Meanwhile, prepare pastry. Blend together flour, baking powder, and margarine. Stir in beaten egg and 1/2 cup (125 mL) water. Roll until 1/2 inch (1 cm) thick. Cover stew with pastry and bake for another 15 minutes.

Photo: Typical rocky coast, Labrador

Pork cakes are a tradition in Grand Bank, on the Burin Peninsula, and they are usually made on Saturdays.

Pork Cakes

6 potatoes
1 cup (250 mL) minced salt pork
2 cups (500 mL) flour
2 tsp (10 mL) baking powder
1 tsp (5 mL) baking soda

Peel and cook potatoes; mash well. Mix in pork. Add flour, baking powder, and baking soda. Mix together with hands and form into cakes. Bake at 400°F (200°C) for 30 minutes to 1 hour or until browned.

Photo: A peaceful harbour

21

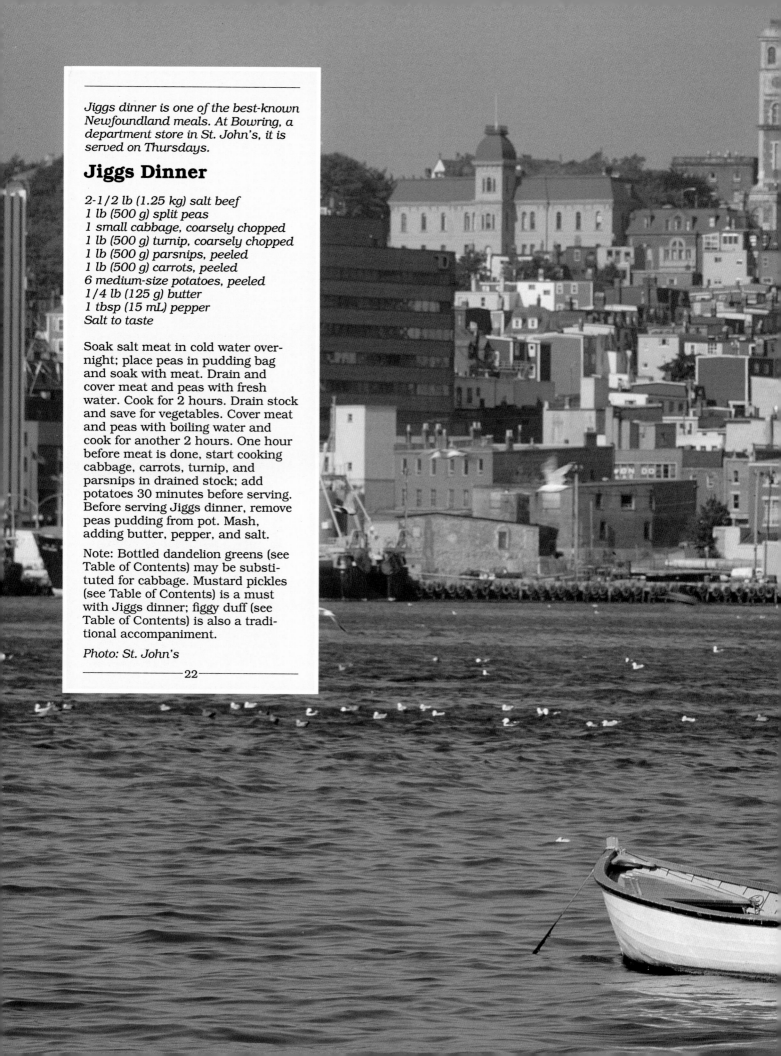

Jiggs dinner is one of the best-known Newfoundland meals. At Bowring, a department store in St. John's, it is served on Thursdays.

Jiggs Dinner

2-1/2 lb (1.25 kg) salt beef
1 lb (500 g) split peas
1 small cabbage, coarsely chopped
1 lb (500 g) turnip, coarsely chopped
1 lb (500 g) parsnips, peeled
1 lb (500 g) carrots, peeled
6 medium-size potatoes, peeled
1/4 lb (125 g) butter
1 tbsp (15 mL) pepper
Salt to taste

Soak salt meat in cold water over-night; place peas in pudding bag and soak with meat. Drain and cover meat and peas with fresh water. Cook for 2 hours. Drain stock and save for vegetables. Cover meat and peas with boiling water and cook for another 2 hours. One hour before meat is done, start cooking cabbage, carrots, turnip, and parsnips in drained stock; add potatoes 30 minutes before serving. Before serving Jiggs dinner, remove peas pudding from pot. Mash, adding butter, pepper, and salt.

Note: Bottled dandelion greens (see Table of Contents) may be substituted for cabbage. Mustard pickles (see Table of Contents) is a must with Jiggs dinner; figgy duff (see Table of Contents) is also a traditional accompaniment.

Photo: St. John's

This was made in logging camps.

Old-Fashioned Baked Beans

2 lb (1 kg) brown-eyed beans
1 medium-size onion, sliced
1/4 cup (50 mL) catsup
1/4 cup (50 mL) brown sugar
3/4 lb (175 g) fat-back pork, sliced
Pinch pepper
1/2 cup (125 mL) molasses
1 tsp (5 mL) dry mustard

Wash beans. Add enough water to cover beans by 2 inches (5 cm). Simmer until skins begin to crack (about 45 minutes). Strain. Combine beans and other ingredients; add water to cover. Place in a deep casserole or crock and bake, covered, at 250°F (125°C) for about 6 hours.

Photo: To lumberjacks and fishermen

This salad is a good way to use up leftover corn.

Pineapple-Corn Salad

1 tin crushed pineapple
2 cups (500 mL) corn kernels
1 tin diced beets
1 or 2 stalks celery, diced
1 cup (250 mL) diced apple
Mayonnaise

Combine all ingredients. Mix well.

Photo: A corn boil

—25—

Increase the amounts as necessary for large get-togethers. There's nothing like a good potato salad at a family picnic.

Old-Fashioned Potato Salad

1/2 cup (125 mL) mayonnaise
1/2 cup (125 mL) minced onion
1 tbsp (15 mL) vinegar
1/2 tsp (2 mL) salt
Pepper to taste
1 hard-boiled egg, chopped
1-1/2 lb (750 g) potatoes, cooked, peeled, and cubed
1 cup chopped celery
Paprika

Stir together first 6 ingredients. Add potatoes and celery, tossing to coat well. Cover and chill for at least 4 hours. Sprinkle with paprika.

Left: Horseback riding
Right: Planting potatoes
Overleaf: Chatting by the wharf

27

These are delicious covered with
butter and molasses.

Grandma's Toutons

Make favourite bread. Pinch off
pieces of leftover dough and fry until
golden brown.

Photo: Burgeo, south coast

Nothing beats warm raisin buns in mid-afternoon or before bedtime.

Tickle-Hour Raisin Buns

3 cups (750 mL) flour
5 tsp (25 mL) baking powder
3/4 tsp (3 mL) salt
5 tbsp (75 mL) butter
1 cup (250 mL) raisins
3 tbsp (50 mL) sugar
2 eggs
2/3 cup (150 mL) milk

Sift together flour, baking powder, and salt. Add butter, raisins, and sugar. Beat together eggs and milk; add to flour mixture. Mix well. Roll on floured board to about 1 inch (2.5 cm) thick. Cut into desired shapes. Bake at 400°F (200°C) until nicely browned.

Left: Harbour Grace, Conception Bay
Right: A solitary boat

Figgy duff sometimes accompanies Jiggs dinner (see Table of Contents). Serve this old favourite with heated molasses.

Auld-Time Figgy Duff

3 cups (750 mL) stale bread crumbs
1 cup (250 mL) raisins
1/2 cup (125 mL) brown sugar
Few grains salt
1 tsp (5 mL) ginger
1 tsp (5 mL) allspice
1 tsp (5 mL) cinnamon
1/4 cup (50 mL) melted butter
3 tbsp (50 mL) molasses
1 tsp (5 mL) baking soda
1 tbsp (15 mL) hot water
1/2 cup (125 mL) flour

Soak bread crumbs in water for a few minutes. Squeeze out and rub between hands; measure. Using a fork, mix together crumbs, raisins, sugar, salt, ginger, allspice, and cinnamon. Add melted butter, molasses, and baking soda, which has been dissolved in 1 tbsp (15 mL) hot water. Add flour and mix well. Pour mixture into damp cheesecloth bag and tie tightly, leaving a little slack to allow for rising. Boil for 1-1/2 hours.

Photo: Island off south coast
Overleaf: Grey River, south coast

Partridgeberries are tart like cranberries, and they can be found on dry barrens throughout the province.

Partridgeberry Bread

1/2 cup (125 mL) margarine
1 cup (250 mL) sugar
2 eggs
1 tsp (5 mL) vanilla
2-1/2 cups (625 mL) flour
2 tsp (10 mL) baking powder

1/4 tsp (1 mL) salt
1/2 cup (125 mL) orange juice
1 cup (250 mL) partridgeberries

Cream together margarine, sugar, and eggs until fluffy. Add vanilla. Combine dry ingredients and fold into creamed mixture alternately with orange juice. Fold in partridgeberries. Pour into greased loaf pan and bake at 350°F (180°C) for 1 hour.

Partridgeberry cottage pudding is best served with a lemon sauce.

Partridgeberry Cottage Pudding

1-3/4 cups (425 mL) sifted flour
2-1/2 tsp (12 mL) baking powder
1/2 tsp (2 mL) salt
1/4 cup (50 mL) shortening
1 tsp (5 mL) vanilla
1 cup (250 mL) sugar
1 egg
2/3 cup (150 mL) milk
1 cup (250 mL) partridgeberries

Sift together flour, baking powder, and salt. Mix together shortening, vanilla, sugar, and egg. Add flour and milk alternately to sugar mixture, beating smooth after each addition. Add partridgeberries and mix in slightly. Pour into greased 8-inch x 8-inch (1-L) pan and bake at 350°F (180°C) for 30 to 40 minutes.

Photo: Freshwater, Placentia Bay
Overleaf: Rocky cliffs

Bakeapples, a tart yellow berry found in wet barrens, are a delicacy in the province.

Barrens Bakeapple Dessert

1/2 cup (125 mL) margarine
1 cup (250 mL) brown sugar
1 cup (250 mL) sifted flour
2 cups (500 mL) rolled oats
1 tsp (5 mL) baking soda
1-1/2 cups fresh bakeapples,
    sweetened

Rub together margarine, sugar, flour, rolled oats, and baking soda until fine and crumbly. Spread half of mixture in bottom of pie plate. Cover with bakeapples. Spread remaining crumb mixture over bakeapples and gently press down until even. Bake at 350°F (180°C) until golden brown. Serve hot.

An average serving of bakeapples contains as much vitamin C as an orange or half a grapefruit. It is said that when the French first settled in Newfoundland and found the berry, they asked, "Baie qu'appelle?" (What is this berry?) And thus answered their own question.

Bakeapple Pie

2 cups (500 mL) bakeapples
1 cup (250 mL) sugar
Pastry
2 tbsp (25 mL) tapioca

Combine bakeapples and sugar; let stand. Meanwhile, prepare pastry. Line bottom of a pie plate with pastry and sprinkle with tapioca to absorb juice. Fill shell with bakeapple mixture and cover with pastry. Bake at 450°F (230°C) for 10 minutes, then 350°F (180°C) for 30 to 40 minutes.

Photo: Gull Island, Conception Bay

This is just as delicious as traditional English trifle but with more kick.

Newfoundland Trifle

2 cups (500 mL) cake cubes
1/3 cup (75 mL) fruit juice or 1/4 cup (50 mL) screech or sherry
2 cups (500 mL) drained sweetened fruit, cut into pieces
2 cups (500 mL) soft custard
Whipped cream
Fruit or toasted almonds for garnish

Divide cake into 6 serving dishes. Dribble juice or screech over cake. Cover with fruit. Pour custard over fruit, and top trifle with whipped cream. Garnish with pieces of fruit or toasted almonds.

Photo: Cabot Tower, St. John's

44

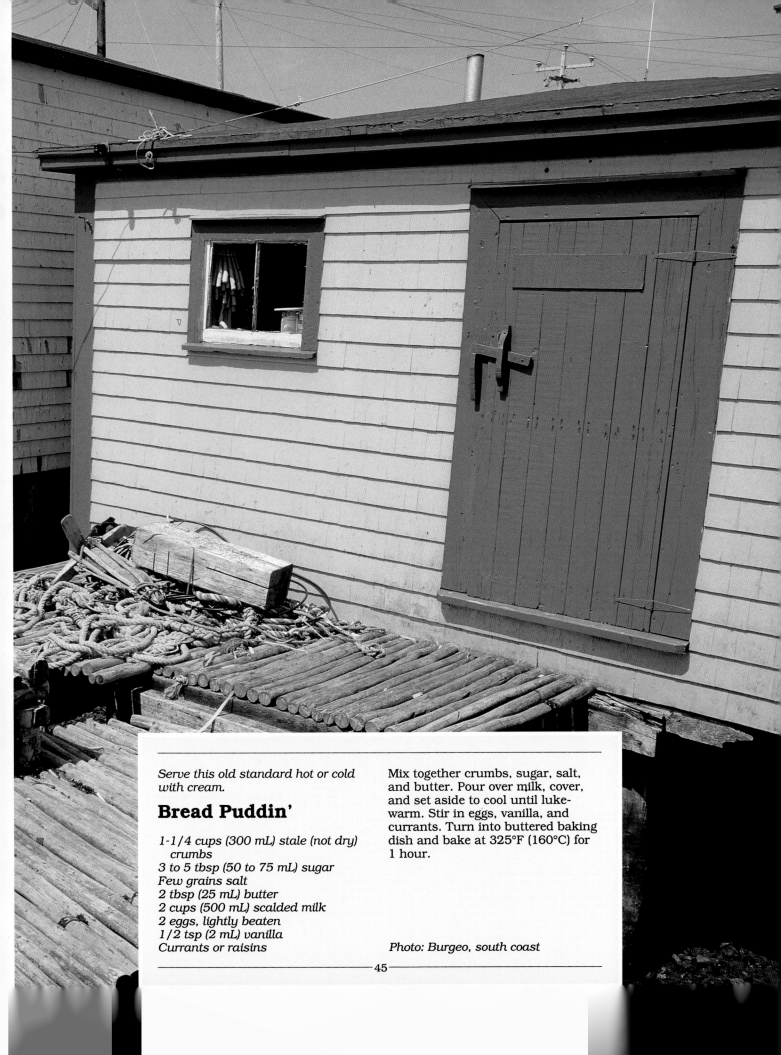

Serve this old standard hot or cold with cream.

Bread Puddin'

1-1/4 cups (300 mL) stale (not dry)
   crumbs
3 to 5 tbsp (50 to 75 mL) sugar
Few grains salt
2 tbsp (25 mL) butter
2 cups (500 mL) scalded milk
2 eggs, lightly beaten
1/2 tsp (2 mL) vanilla
Currants or raisins

Mix together crumbs, sugar, salt, and butter. Pour over milk, cover, and set aside to cool until luke-warm. Stir in eggs, vanilla, and currants. Turn into buttered baking dish and bake at 325°F (160°C) for 1 hour.

Photo: Burgeo, south coast

45

Newfoundland is blueberry heaven.

Blueberry Cobbler

1 qt (1 L) blueberries
1 cup (250 mL) butter
1 cup (250 mL) sugar
3 eggs
1 tsp (5 mL) vanilla
2-1/2 cups (625 mL) flour
3 tbsp (50 mL) baking powder

Place blueberries in a greased loaf pan. Cream butter, adding sugar gradually. Stir in eggs one at a time. Stir in vanilla, flour, and baking powder. Pour mixture over blueberries and bake at 375°F (190°C) for 30 to 40 minutes or until nicely browned.

Newfoundland does not corner the market on fruit desserts, but rhubarb does find its way into many recipes.

Rhubarb Dessert

*3 cups (750 mL) chopped rhubarb
1/4 cup (50 mL) water
3/4 cup (175 mL) sugar
2 tbsp (25 mL) flour*

Combine ingredients and mix well. Place in a greased 9-inch x 9-inch (1.5-L) baking dish. Bake at 350°F (180°C) for 30 to 40 minutes.

*Photo: Hibbs Hole, Conception Bay
Overleaf: Port de Grave, Conception Bay*

This is the province's version of pulled taffy.

Aunt Bessie's Favourite Bull's Eyes

3 tbsp (50 mL) butter
2 cups (500 mL) molasses
1/8 tsp (1 mL) baking soda
2/3 cup (150 mL) sugar
1 tbsp (15 mL) vinegar

Combine all ingredients in a saucepan; stir until sugar is dissolved. Boil to brittle stage and turn into a shallow pan. When cool, pull until light in colour. Using scissors, cut into small pieces.

Photo: Waiting for mom

Believe it or not, fresh cabbage makes delicious pickles.

Fresh-Cabbage Pickles

2 lb (1 kg) cabbage
2 lb (1 kg) onions
1 qt (1 L) vinegar
1 cup (250 mL) sugar
1 tsp (5 mL) salt
1 tbsp (15 mL) curry powder
1 tbsp (15 mL) turmeric

1 tbsp (15 mL) dry mustard
1/2 cup (125 mL) flour
1/2 cup (125 mL) water

Chop cabbage and onions until very fine. Add vinegar and boil for 10 minutes. Add sugar and salt. Combine spices and flour, adding water to form a paste. Stir paste into boiling cabbage and boil for 20 minutes. Pour into hot sterilized jars and seal.

Photo: Root cellar
Overleaf: Long Cove, Placentia Bay

51

Nothing goes better with Jiggs dinner (see Table of Contents) than spicy mustard pickles.

Our Mustard Pickles

*2 cauliflowers
3 or 4 cucumbers
2 lb (1 kg) pickling onions
1/2 cup (125 mL) pickling salt
3 tbsp (50 mL) pickling spices
1/2 cup (125 mL) cold water
3 cups (750 mL) sugar or to taste
1 tbsp (15 mL) dry mustard
1/2 tsp (2 mL) turmeric
5 cups (1.25 L) vinegar
1 tbsp (15 mL) mustard seeds
1 24-oz (750-mL) bottle prepared
    mustard
Flour*

Wash cauliflowers and cucumbers well. Peel onions and cut up cauliflowers and cucumbers. Layer vegetables and pickling salt. Cover and let stand overnight. Drain and thoroughly rinse off pickling salt with cold water. Steep pickling spices in 1/2 cup (125 mL) cold water. Combine sugar, dry mustard, turmeric, vinegar, mustard seeds, and prepared mustard. Stir in spice mixture and vegetables. Cook for 30 minutes. Thicken with flour, pour into hot sterilized jars, and seal.

Rhubarb relish is often eaten with cold canned meats.

Rhubarb Relish

2 qt (2 L) chopped rhubarb
1 qt (1 L) thinly sliced onions
1 pt (500 mL) vinegar
2 cups (500 mL) sugar
1 tbsp (15 mL) salt
1 tsp (5 mL) cloves

1 tsp (5 mL) allspice
1 tsp (5 mL) cinnamon
1 tsp (5 mL) pepper

Combine all ingredients and cook slowly until tender (about 1 hour). Pour into hot sterilized jars and seal.

Photo: Winterton, Trinity Bay

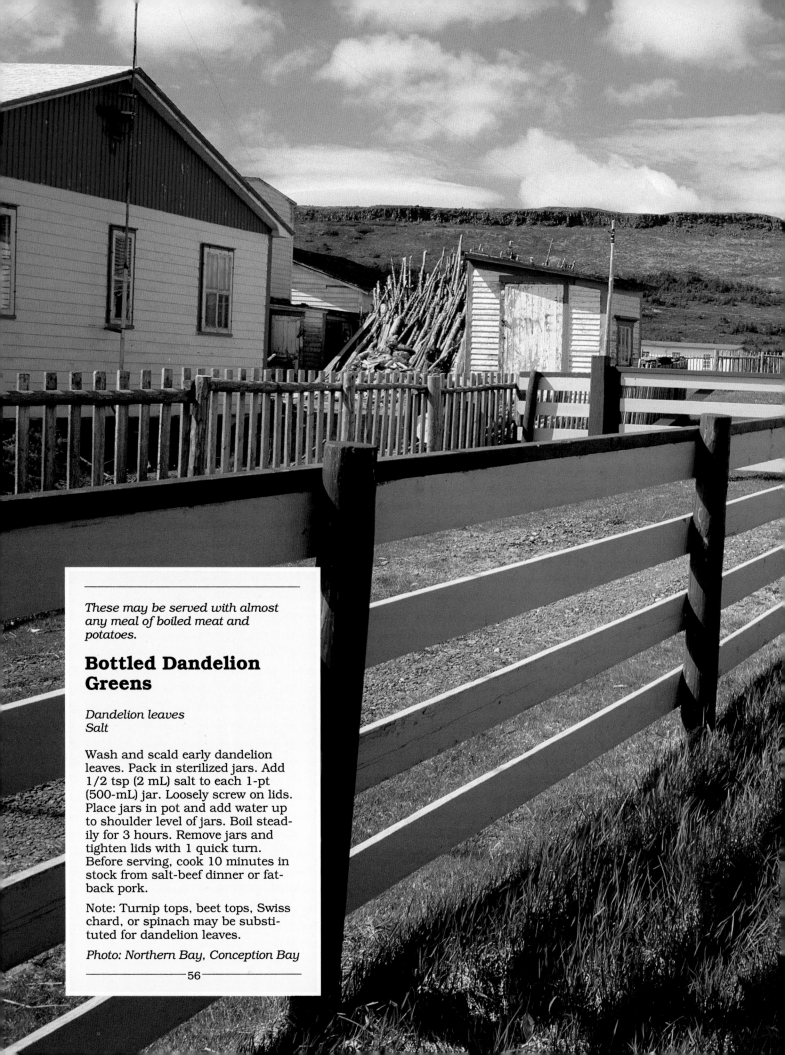

These may be served with almost any meal of boiled meat and potatoes.

Bottled Dandelion Greens

Dandelion leaves
Salt

Wash and scald early dandelion leaves. Pack in sterilized jars. Add 1/2 tsp (2 mL) salt to each 1-pt (500-mL) jar. Loosely screw on lids. Place jars in pot and add water up to shoulder level of jars. Boil steadily for 3 hours. Remove jars and tighten lids with 1 quick turn. Before serving, cook 10 minutes in stock from salt-beef dinner or fatback pork.

Note: Turnip tops, beet tops, Swiss chard, or spinach may be substituted for dandelion leaves.

Photo: Northern Bay, Conception Bay

Squashberries grow on trees, and they make a sweet, red jelly. As they are low in pectin, do not use too much water in this recipe.

Squashberry Jelly

Squashberries
Water
Sugar

Wash squashberries and place in a large pot. Add enough water so that it just covers hand when pressed on berries. Boil until berries are scalded. Strain through a colander. Measure juice and cook 4 cups (1 L) at a time. Cover and bring to a boil. Stir in 1 cup (250 mL) sugar to each cup (250 mL) juice. Boil until a small amount sheets off a metal spoon. Skim off froth and pour into hot sterilized jars and seal.

Left: Typical outport
Right: Grand Beach, Fortune Bay
Overleaf: François, south coast

This wine is well worth the two-month wait required for ageing.

Good Ol' Blueberry Wine

2 qt (2 L) blueberries
4 qt (4 L) boiling water
Sugar
3 cups (750 mL) prunes

Place blueberries in a large pot and add boiling water. Simmer on low heat until begins to boil. Strain. Add 6 cups (1.5 L) sugar to 1 gallon (4 L) juice. Boil for 5 minutes. Cool and add prunes. Pour into crock or jar and cover with cheesecloth. Age 2 months. Strain, bottle, and cork.

Photo: Perry's Cove, Conception Bay

62

Spruce beer is an old Newfoundland beverage, though it is not common now.

Spruce Beer

Black spruce boughs from young
  trees
Water
5 lb (2.5 kg) sugar
1 qt (1 L) molasses
1/4 tsp (1 mL) yeast

Break up spruce boughs and fill a 5-gallon (20-L) pot. Cover with water and boil for 1 hour or until rinds peel easily. Pour water into a 15-gallon (60-L) container; do not strain bits of needles, etc. Add lukewarm water to total 10 to 12 gallons (40 to 48 L). (Pour first couple of gallons over boughs to get all substance.) Add sugar and molasses, stirring until dissolved. Sprinkle yeast on top; do not stir. Let stand in a warm place for about 3 hours, skimming off foam if desired. Strain through gauze cloth, bottle, and cap. Let stand in a warm place for 1 day, then store in fridge or cooler.

Note: Keep bottled beer cold or it could explode.

Photo: Near Belmont
Overleaf: Fishing